Seasons in the Kelp Forest

Written by Jenny Feely

Flying Start
to Literacy®

T0363491

Contents

Introduction

There are seasons in the sea just as there are on land. As the seasons change, so does the sea; cold and rough in winter, warmer and calmer in summer.

The seasons can be seen very clearly in kelp forests, which grow under the sea. As the seasons change, kelp forests and the animals that live in them experience many changes.

holdfast

Kelp holdfasts keep kelp attached to rocks.

Kelp is a thick, brown seaweed that grows from the floor of the ocean up to the surface. When a lot of kelp grows in one area, it forms an underwater forest.

Many plants and seaweeds grow in kelp forests. A lot of animals live there, too. Some eat the kelp and others hide from predators. Some animals lay eggs and raise their young in the shelter of the kelp forest.

How does kelp grow?

Kelp grows from tiny floating spores, which are like seeds. When the spores settle onto rocks, kelp starts to grow. Kelp does not have roots. It has a holdfast that attaches to a rock. The holdfast stops the kelp from floating away.

Kelp does not have leaves. Kelp has blades that look like leaves. And it has a stem called a stipe. The stipe helps the blades to reach the surface of the water.

Some types of kelp also have gas-filled balls called bladders that help the kelp to float up toward the sunlight.

Did you know?

Kelp is not a plant; it is a type of seaweed. It can grow to be more than 53 metres tall.

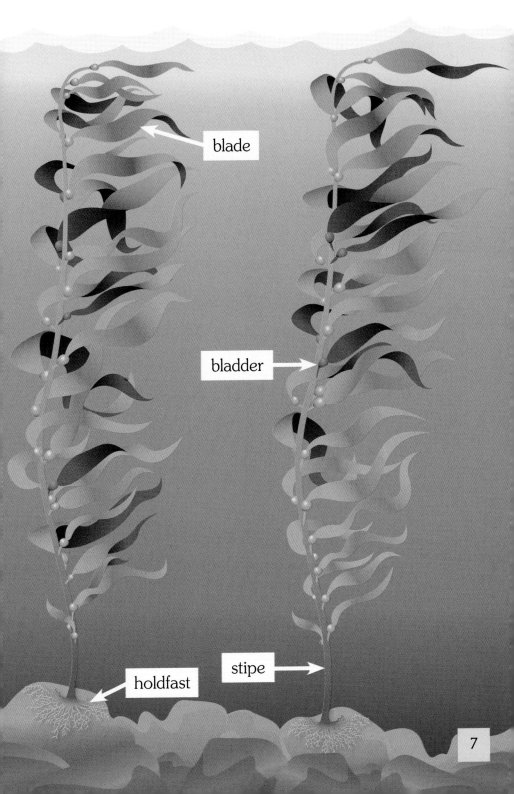

blade

bladder

stipe

holdfast

7

Chapter 1

Winter turns into spring

At the end of winter, there is no kelp forest in the sea – there are only a few broken blades. But thousands of tiny kelp spores float in the water, waiting for spring when the conditions will be right for them to grow.

Did you know?

During late spring, kelp grows at an amazing rate. Giant kelp can grow up to 60 centimetres per day.

How kelp grows

kelp spores

stipes grow toward the surface

spores grow into holdfasts

spores settle on rocks

After the winter storms, the sea is calmer, and the thousands of kelp spores sink to the ocean floor and begin to grow on rocks. The kelp stipes and blades grow toward the water's surface, seeking the energy they need from the sun to keep growing.

Warm nutrient-rich water is perfect for kelp to grow in.

blades and bladders grow

kelp spreads out in a canopy across the water's surface

As the kelp forest starts to grow, many animals return there to eat, lay eggs or raise their young.

The fast-growing kelp is an abundant source of food for grazing animals. As more animals come to the kelp forest to find food, bigger animals come to hunt them.

Sea urchins eat kelp.
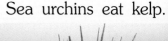

This shark is hunting in the kelp forest.

leafy sea dragon

Kelp forest food web

This food web shows the animals that find food in the kelp forest. Many animals eat kelp.
Sea otters eat the animals that eat kelp.
And sharks hunt sea otters.

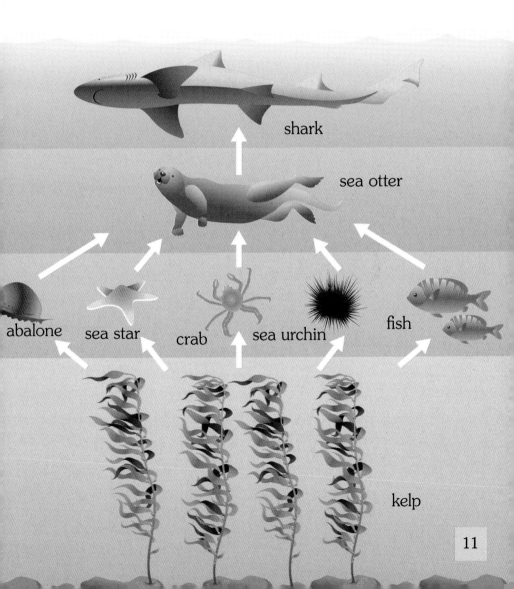

shark

sea otter

abalone   sea star   crab   sea urchin   fish

kelp

Chapter 2

Spring turns into summer

As spring turns into summer, there are fewer nutrients in the water. This means that the growth of the kelp slows. By the time summer comes, the kelp is held up on the surface of the sea by its gas-filled bladders, getting energy from the sun.

gas-filled bladders

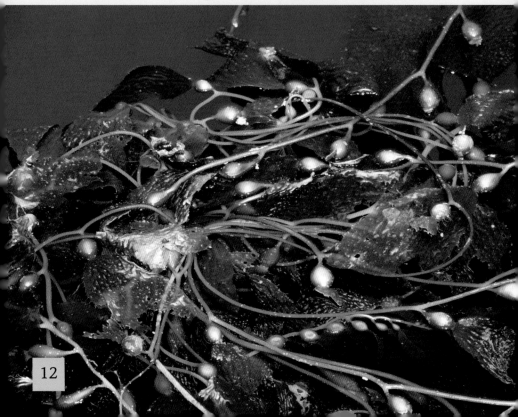

A sea bird is hunting for fish in the kelp blades.

The upper layer of the kelp forest is made up of blades. It is called the canopy, and in summer, the canopy is at its thickest.

Many animals find food and shelter in the canopy of blades. Small animals attach themselves to the kelp blades, and the kelp soon becomes encrusted with them. Small fish hide in the blades and eat the animals that encrust the kelp. Sea birds walk across the kelp blades hunting these fish.

Sea otters live in the kelp forest for most of the year. In summer, they rest in the blades of the canopy. They often wrap themselves in the kelp to stop themselves from drifting away while they sleep. During this time, sea otters raise their pups. The pups remain on the surface, wrapped in kelp, while the mothers dive under the water to look for food.

This sea otter has wrapped itself in kelp.

Some crayfish live in kelp holdfasts.

The canopy of the kelp forest blocks a lot of sunlight from reaching the ocean floor. Here, in the dim light, many animals feed and hide. Crabs, sea stars and sea urchins all live in and around the kelp's holdfasts. Bigger fish swim through the kelp forest.

Did you know?

Kelp holdfasts are such a good home for animals that scientists have recorded more than 23 000 animals living in just five holdfasts.

A sea lion hunts in the kelp forest.

A grey whale passes through the kelp forest.

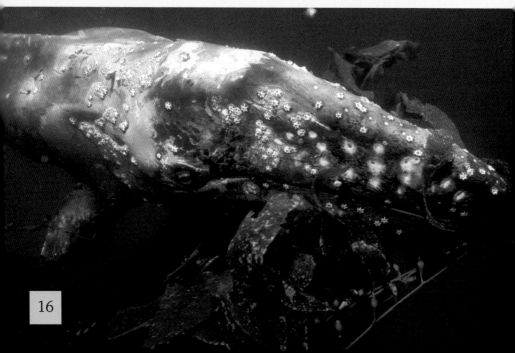

During summer, sea lions, seals and sharks come to hunt the bigger fish that live in the forest. Grey whales also visit the kelp forest. They are usually making their way north, to the Arctic Ocean, but they have been seen to take a mouthful of kelp as they pass through the kelp forest. Sometimes they swim into kelp forests to escape from killer whales that are hunting them.

Some fish that live in the kelp forest lay their eggs there during the summer. The male blacksmith fish makes a place for eggs in the sand. The female lays her eggs there and the male fertilises them, then guards the eggs until they hatch in autumn.

blacksmith fish

Chapter 3

Summer fades into autumn

During autumn, the nutrients in the water get used up. New, warmer water comes to the kelp forest from the open ocean, but there are no nutrients in this water to feed the kelp. The water becomes a lot clearer without these nutrients.

The thick canopy of kelp stops sunlight from reaching the bottom of the sea, preventing new kelp plants from growing. In autumn, there are also fewer hours of sunlight each day, so the kelp gets less energy from the sun and grows more slowly.

It is very dark in the kelp forest in autumn.

Blacksmith fish leave the kelp forest.

Many of the fish and other animals that began life in the kelp forest are now big enough to leave it. No longer needing its shelter, they leave to search for food in other parts of the ocean.

Did you know?

Newly hatched blacksmith fish sometimes travel over 400 kilometres from the kelp forest.

A jellyfish floats through the kelp.

There is still some life in the kelp forest
during autumn. Jellyfish float through the kelp.
Rockfish and sunfish swim along the edges
of the kelp forest, looking for food. Many
sea otters breed during autumn, so male sea
otters are busy looking for mates.

Chapter 4

Autumn sinks into winter

As autumn ends and winter begins, the kelp
forest is torn apart. Wild storms bring
huge waves that toss and tear at the kelp.
A lot of kelp is torn from rocks and carried
along by the waves, uprooting other kelp
in its path.

The horn shark stays in the kelp forest during winter.

As the winter storms come again and again, there is less and less kelp. With less kelp to eat and shelter in, many animals move to other parts of the ocean.

But some stay. Horn sharks mate and lay their eggs. The female horn shark wedges them into cracks in the rocks or digs holes in the sand for the eggs. In winter, sea otter pups learn to hunt with their mothers.

Ocean storms are important for coastal animals. The torn and uprooted kelp is pushed onto the coast by the storms. Kelp that washes up onto beaches provides food for the many animals that live there.

Kelp is washed up on the beach.

When the kelp is torn out of the kelp forest, it makes room for new kelp to grow. Some of the torn kelp blades settle on the ocean floor, where they are either eaten by animals or rot. These animals' droppings and the rotting kelp release nutrients into the water. The nutrients settle on the ocean floor during winter. When spring comes, these nutrients will help new kelp to grow.

The underwater cycle

The four seasons form a cycle underwater, just as they do on land. Each season brings different changes to the kelp forest, and these could not happen without the changes before them. All the seasons are equally important for a healthy kelp forest.

winter

autumn  spring

summer

Glossary

abundant a large amount; more than enough

animal droppings the waste from an animal's body

bladder a gas-filled ball on kelp that helps the plant to float to the surface

canopy a thick layer of kelp that floats on the surface of the water

encrusted covered with

gas-filled full of gas; air is a type of gas

grazing eating small amounts of food frequently

holdfast the root-like part of kelp that attaches the kelp to rocks

nutrient-rich healthy food, filled with vitamins and minerals

predator an animal that hunts and kills other animals for food

spore a tiny speck made up of cells

A note from the author

I got the idea for this book from watching a television program called *The Blue Planet.* One episode of the series explored a year under the sea, looking at the changes that occurred as the seasons changed.

It had never occurred to me that there would be seasons under the sea, so I began to research this further. I found that some of the most profound seasonal changes happen in kelp forests.

I found a lot of useful information on the websites of the National Marine Sanctuaries and the Monterey Bay Aquarium.